# STILL LIVING IN TOWN

# STILL LIVING IN TOWN

Kevin FitzPatrick

MIDWEST VILLAGES & VOICES

Some of these poems have appeared in the following magazines, anthologies, and other media: *Art Word Quarterly, Lowertown Reading Jam Series* (Saint Paul Neighborhood Network), *North Coast Review, The North Stone Review, Saint Paul Almanac, Small Press Review, Spout,* and *War and Strife* (Cracked Walnut Press).

Midwest Villages & Voices
Post Office Box 40214
Saint Paul, MN 55104

midwestvillages@yahoo.com

*For Meridel, Rachel, and Gayla*

# CONTENTS

ONE: SHOVELING WOOD CHIPS

Blackberries  11
Trailering Vino  12
Agreement  13
Seventy Chickens  14
Shoveling Wood Chips  16
Her Right Hand  17
Country Visiting  18
In Dreams  19
Carronay  20
Lambing  22
The Road Home  24

TWO: IN TRANSIT

In Transit  27
For Sale  28
Come Again  30
Say, Pal  32
Banana Sale  33
Expecting  34
Scabs  36
Wellstone, Senator Wellstone!  38
Immigrants  40
Green Revelry  42
Survivor  44
Time Piece  45
Trust  46

THREE: TROUBLE KNOCKING

The Other Side  49
Hurry, Hurry  50
Getting Around  51
Tending the Burn Pile  52
Leashes  53

Cowboy  54
Coyotes  56
Cast Room  57
Harvest Time  59
Scheduled  61
Easement  63
Stella  65
Run-up to Tina's Election Loss  67
Trouble Knocking  68
Hobby Farm  69

FOUR: STAYING PUT

Overtime  73
Up  74
June Afternoon  75
The Easy Part  76
Midwinter Thaw  77
Ties That Bind  79
Memento  80
Mohs Surgery Waiting Room  81
Valentine's Day  82
Navigator, Next  83
Questioning  85
Bobcat Skid-Steer Loader  86
Farewell  88
Good Hay  90
Staying Put  91
Giddyup  92

# ONE

# SHOVELING WOOD CHIPS

# BLACKBERRIES

I choose "Blackberry-Picking" to read to Tina,
a poem by Nobel prize winner Seamus Heaney.
I want to support her, show her I accept
her moving back to the country
after years of living in the city with me.
As in Heaney's poem, she too has blackberries
growing wild along the borders of her fields.

But as I read to her how the poet
uses milk cans, pea tins, jam pots
to drop his picked berries in, she interrupts,
"Milk cans are too big—he'll crush them.
He needs berry boxes."

I smile and continue to read
until the poet unloads his berries in a bath
and bemoans a fungus that sets in year after year
to foul the treasure he's picked.
"I wouldn't wash wild berries," Tina says.
"I'd freeze them or put them up right away.
Pick off any insects or thorns,
then freeze them or put them up—make jams, jellies,
pies, juice, wine—they'll rot if you don't."

I don't know who to freeze or put up:
Nobel prize winner Seamus Heaney,
whose poetry I love and admire,
or Tina, who I also love and admire
and who's a three-time Mille Lacs area
4-H grand canning champion.

# TRAILERING VINO

Vino, Tina's Belgian draft horse, dwarfs
the other riding horses. A man paces near us
in the trailering area. He's dusty, sweaty, wears
a cowboy hat, brim down like a country music singer,
and makes some mumbled comment
about loading a big thing like that
as if he expects Vino to bolt.
I watched earlier when Tina was out riding
as he dragged his horse into a trailer.

"Come on, Vino," Tina coaxes. "Step up.
Into the trailer, boy. You can do it."
He is a ninth grade phy-ed swimmer
stuck atop the high diving board
as his classmates dress in the locker room,
having long ago satisfied their requirement.
Tina holding Vino's halter rope
climbs into the trailer and calls,
"It's not scary, boy. See?
Come on in. Just step up."

I think of Niles who trained Vino advising us,
"Never load a horse when you're rushed."
I have our poodle, Katie, leashed and sitting quietly
as I stand at Vino's backside flicking strands
of his long cream-colored tail against his rump,
an annoyance like flies
he'll hopefully move forward from.
I don't care what the cowboy-looking character thinks.
Vino steps up and into the trailer.

# AGREEMENT

Our work today, our second day of haying,
is all that's on Tina's mind.
She doesn't even mention breakfast,
which is usually a lengthy, delicious event
since I'm only out to her farm on weekends.
Katie noses her empty dog dish
and Peter won't quit meowing.

But it's Vino who gets her attention
by kicking the metal stable gate.
His clanging always unsettles her
as it starts Katie barking.
"Will you give the horse some oats?" Tina asks.
"Sure, and I'll feed the dog and cat,
but what about breakfast?"
"We'll eat after we stack those bales in the barn;
the wagons have to be empty when Swenson comes."
"Don't forget our agreement," I tell her.
"There's a couple hundred bales."

"Are you still mulling over that Irish movie
where the woman brings out lunch
to her husband and son haying
and has a heart attack and dies?"
"Yes," I say, "and then the two discuss
whether to bring her back to the house
or finish haying first. We've agreed
if one of us collapses out here
the other calls for help at once."

"Well, she was dead," Tina responds,
"so what did it matter if they left her there?
The hay could be ruined if it rained."

# SEVENTY CHICKENS

As I drive into the farm,
Tina is coaxing a frantic chicken
out of the lower limbs of a pine tree.
The bird that Tina raised from a chick
trusts her and comes out.
She strokes the chicken in her arms
and hands it to her neighbor Janelle
who scolds, "Now stop it, do you hear?"
as if it were a misbehaving pet,
then hauls it to the killing post
and slits its throat.

The slaughter of seventy chickens
on a cool, rainy, July day has begun.
I've taken time off from work to help,
though Tina warned I might not like it.
"You didn't grow up on a farm."
"No," I said, "but I eat chicken."
Janelle and her husband, Stan, do the killing
then strip the feathers using
scalding water and a motorized plucker.
Tina cuts off the head, pulls
any remaining feathers, and guts it.
I brush and hose the cavity
and drop the carcass into icy water.

Warm flesh smell pervades the shed.
After several hours I go into the house
cold and in need of coffee.
It appears our work is done.
Janelle and Stan come in. They are amazed
how big Tina's chickens are,
that she only lost a few raising them.
Janelle sees my numb look and offers
that chickens are creatures low
on the food chain of being
whose purpose is to feed humans.

I am about to say I'll never eat chicken again
when Tina comes in requesting we cut up,
package, and freeze the birds before dark,
but we can wash, disinfect, and put away
the killing post, feather plucker,
knives, tables, bins, and dispose
the heads, blood, and entrails in the morning.

# SHOVELING WOOD CHIPS

I think of James Wright's poem, "Lying in a Hammock
at William Duffy's Farm in Pine Island, Minnesota,"
the poet reclining in mystical bliss
through late afternoon and early evening.
I suggested we buy a weekend retreat
when Tina talked of needing a change:
a lake cabin without power or running water
where we'd fish, read, doze, and never mow the lawn.

She envisioned an eighty-acre farm with animals,
fruit trees, large gardens with vegetables,
grapes, berries, alfalfa fields for hay,
woodlands for fuel, a way of life.

I am shoveling another load of wood chips
on a Saturday afternoon, pulling the cart up the road
to dump it over the path Vino erodes
trudging from the pasture up to the barn.

We just corked one hundred bottles of wine
from last year's harvest of currant,
raspberry, blueberry, grape. Her two
freezers are crammed with this year's berries

and now the grapes need picking.
Tina's anxious. I'll tell her I'll quit my job,
move out here, tie a hammock between two oaks,
drink wine, eat grapes, whatever it takes.

# HER RIGHT HAND

I often feared Tina might get hurt out here
working on the farm, but never thought
we'd be standing side by side when it happened,
when some metal piece dropped two stories down
from the stainless steel chimney we were cleaning,
whacking, bloodying her middle knuckle,
an injury she shook off for days
until her whole right hand swelled up.

I insisted she see a doctor,
but Tina kept working—haying, stacking wood,
canning vegetables, racking wine, training her horses.
"You need two hands to live out here," I said.
"If I go to a doctor," she huffed,
"I'll get better in two weeks.
If I don't, I'll get better in fourteen days."

I insisted she see a doctor
after watching her in bed in the dark
stare at her red swollen hand,
after hearing her yelp during chores
when Katie chasing a squirrel brushed against her,
after I became the right hand she needed
to winterize the farm equipment.

I was slow and clumsy changing spark plugs,
draining fluids, adjusting belts, sharpening blades.
Tina agreed to see a doctor.
He warned she could lose her hand, took X-rays,
prescribed antibiotics, hot packs,
slowly brought the swelling down,
slowly cured the infection,
saved our lives on the farm.

## COUNTRY VISITING

A knock at dusk brings our final visitors.
Six or seven children, dressed in orange
and each wielding a real rifle, call out,
"Thank you for letting us deer hunt. Thank you."
Jill, who had stopped to return a saddle,
then stayed for coffee and rhubarb crisp,
leaves warily.

People have come and gone all afternoon:
the tax assessor stopped on seeing
the new red-metal animal shelter.
A nearby cattle farmer pitched a deal
to hay Tina's fields next year.
Then a retired couple living now in California
posed Tina and Katie for a photo by the pump.
"Who'd ever believe a farm dog poodle?" they asked.

Sometime well into this afternoon of visitors
I reflect that I've driven two hours to get here
and have sat, talked, and eaten rhubarb crisp repeatedly
until I feel like a reenactor at a historical museum.

In the city I screen visitors in and out
through my front and back door peepholes.
Tina's doors are glass. If I were to move out here,
perhaps I could hire these orange-clad children
to arm a checkpoint at the farm's entrance.

As they relive for us today's hunt—
a wisp of a girl shot the first deer—
I wave to their parents waiting up by the mailbox
and wonder if they'd have time for some rhubarb crisp.

# IN DREAMS

The doorbell rings and rings.
I get up but by then intruders huddle
behind the living room curtains.
I strike them with a chair
and holler so loudly I wake
to Katie barking and all
the metal things around the farm
squeaking and creaking through
the chilly, windy night.

Katie comes over to me from her bed
and stations herself sitting toward the door.
I hear you dreaming through all this,
chattering to someone about making jam.
I decide not to wake you to ask
what you would do out here alone
if a stranger actually rang
the doorbell late at night.

Your dream talk calms Katie.
She turns and turns and turns
descending gently onto her side
and soon is chasing something in her dream,
her paws tapping against the floorboard.

I dream I'm parked in a garage that has no driveway
but a drop-off ten feet down.
I've parked here to protect my car
from raccoons scratching the finish.
How did I get in here?
I hear people coming.
How do I get out?

# CARRONAY

The storm the weather people scared us with all winter
hit for real on a Monday morning in the middle of March:
high winds pushed a foot of snow into three-foot drifts.
I was stuck on the farm until the plows came,
unable to drive back to the city to work.

The horses and sheep were content with oats and hay;
the dogs wrestled outside, then settled in the mud room,
nibbling off chunks of snow from their legs and paws;
birds at the feeders—bluejays, cardinals, woodpeckers,
goldfinches, nuthatches, chickadees—chased each other off
as if it were a normal work day.

I looked out the kitchen bay window and sipped tea.
Tina was in the cellar checking, I assumed,
the carrots stored in bins of sawdust since last fall.
She had yelled up the stairs last weekend
as if the cellar were flooding,
"We have to do something fast!
The carrots are sprouting!
Do you know anybody at work who cooks or bakes?
They're good in stew, soup, meat loaf—
almost anything—cakes, muffins."
I found a few takers at work for a dozen of these
dirt-crusted, enormous, muscular carrots,
photogenic in the sense they mirrored our toil
tilling, planting, watering, weeding, harvesting.

I had planned to take another dozen to work
when Tina appeared in the kitchen with a bin full.
"Will you help me make carrot wine today?
I tried that wine I made two years ago for the first time.
It's like a fine chardonnay. I couldn't believe it.
I'll call it carronay—but don't tell anyone it's carrot."

The storm outside swept through the kitchen
as I lugged up fifty pounds of carrots
and Tina like a magician brought out lemons, limes,
oranges, peppercorns, pounds of sugar, kettles,
graters, mashers, straining bags and plastic buckets.
I looked at my cup of tea on the kitchen table.
I looked out the bay window.
I knew she was German when I met her,
but why couldn't I have met a book-reading German?

## LAMBING

Tina's ewe had started labor earlier then stopped.
Her neighbors drove over when she phoned
and climbed into the pen to help birth her first lambs.
Jim searched the ewe with hands slick with liquid soap.
"There's the head. And the front legs.
Rose, should I bring it out?" he asked.
"No, I'd give it more time."

Their lantern lit up the shelter late
on a rainy Saturday night in May.
Rose wore a pair of shiny green dress shoes.
Years ago they raised their family on this farm.
"I could stand on the front steps or back,"
Jim told us once, "and all I could see was work."

A black lamb was born first, sliding wet
and limp onto the hay strewn earth
like something discarded.
Jim cleared its throat and nostrils.
A white lamb emerged and in minutes the two
were up and squirming out of the pen. I turned
them back and secured the base with bales of hay.

Lambs need to nurse shortly after birth
and might not figure it out when born at night.
Jim and Tina held the ewe against the shelter wall.
Rose put her finger in the black lamb's mouth,
made sucking sounds, then placed it on the ewe's teat.
The lamb's tail wagged like a meter dial gone wacky.
Soon the white one was nursing too.

The next morning Tina had to be away.
The lambs curled in the hay appeared too weak
to rise and reach their distant mother.
I thought of Rose's shiny green shoes for good luck
and climbed into the pen to hold the ewe in place
and alternate the lambs on her teats.

I recalled a friend's comment when I complained
about all the work I did when Tina first moved to her farm.
"It's not something you would have chosen," he said.
It wasn't, but that morning on my knees
in the piss-soaked and poop-laden hay,
I was happy to be there,
feeling the lambs liven,
tails wagging.

# THE ROAD HOME

Thud! A deer careens off my car's hood
then bolts into a ditch. My front end is crunched,
the radiator leaking fluid. A stranger
with a cell phone becomes a sheriff
relieved the deer has disappeared
so he doesn't have to delve into
the tick-filled brush to shoot it. The sheriff
becomes a tow truck driver missing
his left leg and most of his right hand
who lowers a wheelchair from his truck's cab
and drops down into it to maneuver
chains here and chains there to haul
my crumpled car up onto the flatbed.

I bum a ride with him back to Minneapolis.
The tow truck's windshield has multiple cracks;
the seat belt-less cab is bouncy and loud,
muffling my inquiries into what all this means.
A few blocks from my home, after crossing
the Lake Street bridge over the Mississippi,
the tow truck nicks a teenager,
the last in a band of bicyclists
racing through a red light.
As I get out to help him,
he's back on his bike pedaling madly away,
intact and intent on catching his friends,
deer disappearing down a familiar alley.

# TWO

# IN TRANSIT

# IN TRANSIT

Sunday afternoon
I stop at Cannon's on Lake Street
on my drive back to the city from Tina's farm.
I place a box of work boots on the counter
then search my pockets for Tina's receipt,
pulling out twine, hay, twigs, cockleburs,
and dead ladybugs before finding it.

The clerk looks over this stuff,
looks over my unshaven face,
duct tape holding my down vest together,
dirt on my faded blue jeans,
and says, "We don't take back worn boots."
I tell her the person I'm returning them for
lives in Wisconsin and has assured me
she's only walked on carpet with them.
The boots are too tight.

"These boots are worn," she says opening the box
and calls over a burly man stationed
like a bouncer at the front door.
He nods support. I ask to see the manager.
"There ain't no manager today," she says.
"Come back Monday."

I'm back one hour later after driving home
and calling Tina who called the store. The manager
wherever he was earlier heard her loud and clear
ninety miles over the telephone.
He accepts the boots and refunds her money
as I stand before him shaven,
wearing clean black jeans,
and the coat I'll wear to the office tomorrow.

## FOR SALE

I note as I approach Wally and Ken
facing each other in the parking lot
that Wally's service station is up for sale,
that my Mercury Comet hasn't moved since yesterday,
that I am a customer here, not a referee.
I overhear Wally tell Ken, "Keep walking."
"Dad," Ken replies, "I'm going to walk,
but you didn't tell me to walk."
"Just keep walking," Wally says.
"I'm going to walk, but you didn't tell me to walk."

The phone rings. Wally cursing hurries inside.
Ken tells me he can't change my points
and distributor cap. He's sorry.
He's picking up a rental truck. He's late.
He's bought a service station up north.
I go inside. Wally rips into me
how Ken can fix cars, but I wouldn't know
a distributor cap from a bottle cap.
I've heard this before, so I don't quip,
"Why doesn't Ken buy your station then?"

Yesterday Wally drove out
to start my car in the rain. He couldn't jump it,
so he pushed my car with his tow truck
up and down and around the local streets.
I'd pop the clutch when he'd honk,
but the engine wouldn't turn over.
Wally blared at me when we reached his station
that every American male growing up
should learn to fix a car. His son sure did.
But later he phoned me elated
as if he'd found a treasure hunt's gold medallion:
"You have a tiny crack in your distributor cap
where moisture has been seeping in.
Damn it to hell, I found your problem."

Now Ken drives off.
I tell Wally, "I can bus to work.
My points and distributor cap can wait."
Wally is a month out of the hospital.
His joints froze up this winter from working under cars
in the cold damp pit he climbs down into.
He relaxes some and tells me to call him tomorrow.
I am the enigmatic son he never had.

## COME AGAIN

At my first haircut by Johnny Peterson
he was as terse as the sign in his window:
Men Women
FLATTOPS
Done Your Way.

"Do many women get flattops?" I asked.
"Sure, a lot of them are cops."
"I'd just like a trim," I tell him.
"How trim? I can cut hair off, but I can't put it back on."
Johnny said little more during my haircut.
I thought at eighty years old or so
he might be hard of hearing,
but when I asked why Margaret's,
the café across the street, had closed,
he quipped, "She talked too much."

But Rod, the roly-poly used-car dealer next door,
talked enough for the two of them.
He sat in the other barber chair
eating lunch and sipping a glass of beer.
"Johnny and I were orphans.
I was raised by Swedes and Johnny by Norwegians,
but, you won't believe this, we're both Irish."

The front door opened again:
the used-car customers knew Rod was there.
"I'll take it," a woman with a baby said.
Rod had a FREE CAR sign on a Ford Tempo,
but to get it you had to say the magic words.
All through my haircut people had come in warily:
"Does it run?"
"Why are you giving it away?"
"Can I see the maintenance record?"
"Does it have an engine?"
"I'll take it" must have been the magic words
as Rod got down from the chair and left.

"Come again,"
Johnny Peterson, the Irish barber, called to me.
I have, and I've learned
during one of his more loquacious haircuts
he's sober now and single
but on excellent terms
with each of his former wives.

## SAY, PAL

The driver I beat out for that last pump
might rightfully lean on his horn and roar,
and I at such close range instinctively
would stick my fist out, cursing him.
Instead, he holds his hand palm up as if
to show he's weaponless and means no harm.
I think of Francis of Assisi's hand,
a landing place, a trusted perch for birds.
Emerging from my car to pump some gas,
I call, "Say, pal, I won't take long."

## BANANA SALE
*At Downtown Fruit & Vegetable Company*

FIVE POUNDS! ONE BUCK!
I pick a firm banana out for lunch
and walking to the scale,
I ask a little, balding man,
"How much for one?"

Pulling at his green apron,
chomping on his cigar,
he pats my back and barks,
"Oh take the miserable thing."

# EXPECTING

*Thursday, May 28:*
"I've got a baby girl!" Ann tells me
as she runs across to my cubicle.
"A four-month-old baby girl.
That was the social worker calling.
Don't ever tell Henry I told you first.
I'm not ready for her. It's not the time.
I expected her maybe in a year or so.
I've got to call Henry, but I'm telling Beth now."

*Friday, May 29:*
She phones her brother and her sister and her mother.
"I'm not ready for her. It's not the time.
Nathan's only three. Henry's changing jobs."
"You just do it," her mother says. "It all works out."
At noon she picks up baby-girl clothes at Kathy's house.
Later she calls the foster parents.
The man knew who she was right away:
they've had seventeen foster babies.

"Did they invite you to see her?"
"No. There's quite a ceremony when she's delivered.
They've bought a pink ruffled outfit for her.
She's eighteen pounds and smiley, rolls over a lot,
and is a good sleeper. He was about to feed her.
She feeds six times a day. 'Great,' I said to him,
'a little girl with a big appetite.'
I was kidding. I was only kidding."

*Monday, June 1:*
Ann visited her baby this weekend.
She couldn't hold off until the ceremony.
"I took about three dozen pictures.
They call her 'Princess' and 'Sweetie'
so she doesn't respond to a name that'll change.
We're thinking of Laura or Elizabeth. Emily maybe.
Her birth mother called her Bobbi Jo."

*Thursday, June 4:*
Ann's quiet this morning and seems tired.
Her desk is stacked with work. Is she still thinking
she's not ready for her, it's not the time?
At ten she switches to her contact lenses and says,
"I'm picking up Elizabeth." "Elizabeth?" I ask.
"Yes, finally. I've been driving across town all week
to help the foster parents after work.
They've got two babies, kids of their own,
and the house is a mess."

It is the time.
It's time for Elizabeth.

## SCABS

A born-and-raised-in-Minnesota Democrat,
I never thought to cross the picket line.
When the union called, I signed up
for the dawn loading-dock picket crew.
"Just get the names of those who cross.
Someone will phone their homes at night."

Scabs scurried to the loading dock door
later in the strike's first week
when the normal entrances had picketers like Ted,
the Polish ex-cop from Chicago, who'd taunt,
"This isn't Walmart, Al, you fat, friggin' twerp."

Still, I did challenge scabs that first week:
"Rick, will you join us today?"
"I've decided to do what's best for me."
"Craig, will you join us today?"
"I've got a wedding to pay for."
"Sheila, will you join us today?"
"I will maybe next week."
As the second week hardened, I called
to the Ricks and Craigs and Sheilas,
"Why don't you go in a real door?"

Our first day back Carla from the Iron Range
stormed into Bonnie's American flag-draped cubicle
and roared, "Your crossing stabbed us in the back!"
Bonnie in tears pled new car payments.
Carla yelled their clerical jobs—
now no more than stuffing envelopes—
wouldn't exist without the union
fighting for upgrades in their duties.

Ted during the strike worried we'd settle cheap
and go back in with our dicks hanging out.
We got a minimal raise
but stopped deep cuts in medical.
Ted says he'll never talk to scabs.
I'll say "hello" but never "how are you?"

## WELLSTONE, SENATOR WELLSTONE!
*In my sister Ellen's voice*

I didn't talk about him much when he was alive:
he was so strong on the issues—
health care, welfare, war, abortion—
I'd just get into arguments out here.
So I didn't realize how much I missed him,
how much Paul Wellstone represented me.

The last time I saw him was in our Pioneer Days parade,
the summer before the plane crash.
I couldn't get my husband or boys to go with me;
they said it was too hot, as usual.
I sat on the hill away from the crowds,
but as the parade got going full gear,
some people I've seen at school meetings settled in,
a glum bunch opposed to any sex education.
They'd solve all our social woes
with spending cuts and more freeways
so they could move farther and farther out.

The high school band marched by,
the Vulcans from St. Paul leaped from their fire engine,
scattering the crowd with threats of grease paint kisses,
Shriners in their fez hats, teams of draft horses,
and then our representative to the state legislature
sitting atop a new yellow convertible.
I call her our home-schooling queen.
She's schooled all her children at home
and thinks she's an expert in education.
Her campaign aides ran ahead with literature
and those around me jostled for it.

When Paul's green bus came chugging along behind,
they all sat still as stones and wouldn't take his literature.
I couldn't just sit there. I jumped up and yelled,
"Wellstone, Senator Wellstone!" He waved
to all of us from the platform at the back of his bus,
then moments after he passed, he looked toward me
and mouthed the words, "Thank you."

# IMMIGRANTS

The historic Dahl house
that the governor called ugly
and plucked out of sight
to construct a finance building
is high and dry on cement blocks
and circled by a chain link fence
in a corner of the lot where I park.
The back of this working-class cottage
is draped with blue tarp; the roof
missing shingles; fascia
and other trim hanging loose;
windows and doors boarded over.

An Irish immigrant carpenter
built it for hire in 1858.
Now a century-and-a-half later
I get out of my car each morning
to see this house the governor disparaged
and see in the same span to the west,
high above downtown, the Cathedral of St. Paul,
whose construction an archbishop, the son
of the immigrant carpenter, dreamed and oversaw.

There's an encampment beneath the freeway overpass
on the terraced hill leading toward the cathedral
and the Minnesota History Center.
At noon today three young Latino men
climbed up from there and over
the high, black wrought-iron fence
that lines the freeway overpass.
They could have been men who roofed my house
or cleaned my office cubicle.

They were at the bottom of a long set of steps
I descended hurriedly back to work.
A city crew had come to clear their encampment.
I imagined the Dahl house bestowed
to these homeless, scattering men,
a musing even in these political times
not as farfetched as the dream
of an immigrant carpenter's son.

## GREEN REVELRY

They wave to me in joy and welcoming,
the great parade of green-clad merrymakers
on holiday from Lent and winter's grip
to celebrate St. Patrick's Day downtown.
But then I check my watch—lunch hour is up.
I fasten my ID and back at work
our windowless guard asks into the mike
whether the sun's still out then buzzes me in.
Later, as I plod the blocks to where I park,
I pass a party where no one is there:
a table, four chairs, cards and cigarettes,
green beer in mugs, a grill with red hot coals,
a boom box thundering sad country songs,
hats and coats flung across the melting yard.

I'm not surprised no one's around. I've been
to Waverly on St. Patrick's Day. I bet
they're on a break from their shenanigans
like Uncle Red. He'll sing, tell stories, dance,
and drink from what he calls his doctor's kit.
Such revelry in time will wear Red down
and flopping on a chair he'll snooze, but soon,
as if a bell has rung, he'll rise renewed
to sing and dance a round of "Nickolina."
Then Dan, proud bearer of the shamrock banner,
will start the march of "McNamara's Band"
out of the KC Hall to Jimmy Fitz's bar
where they'll parade in style in crazy hats
from derbies to berets to coonskin caps
drawn from Aunt Colleen's great bottomless bag,
and Red beneath a green-plumed admiral's hat
will launch into "Ist Das Nicht Ein Schnitzelbank?",
then marching back, swapping and snatching hats,
they'll polka to the O'Szyplinski band.

At ten they'll toast the Irish Honor Roll
recalling our departed relatives,
their names on large green stars across one wall.
"John FitzPatrick," Dan will proclaim, and toward
that smoky sky they'll all call out, "Hear, hear"
and drink. "Eliza Walsh, his wife." "Hear, hear"
for my great grandmother born in County Mayo.
"Hear, hear" to names of kinfolk more have known
like Joe Borell and Frank and Florence Padden,
until "Hear, hear" for Duly Herbst, my aunt,
who just last year had served us sloppy joes.
Then her son, Dan, her daughters, Mary Kay and Ann,
will lead the march of "McNamara's Band"
rollicking out the door toward Jimmy Fitz's bar.

## SURVIVOR

Ray and I lift my father
and position him in his walker
for the one-hundred-foot trek
from the dining area to his room.
Ray grips the belt on the back of my father's pants;
I steady my father's right hand with my left.
He takes five or six quick, one-inch steps
then veers off like a self-propelled toy
and has to be stopped and turned.

I am a visitor to the nursing home.
My father is eighty-nine years old and failing
but doesn't want a wheelchair.
Ray, an aide about fifty, is Filipino
and talks to him now in a language
I assume is his native tongue.
My father, a Bataan Death March survivor,
answers in short responses
I am unable to understand.

Ray and I shuffle as we work him
around the corner and into his room.
We let him down slowly into a chair
where it will be easier for Ray
to wash him and change him to pajamas.
My father smiles and utters something
in the language they share. Ray replies
and then, as he combs my father's hair, says,
"You're my buddy, Mr. FitzPatrick."

Later, I ask Ray was it Pilipino or Spanish,
the language they were speaking?
"No, no," he says. "It's Japanese.
Your father is teaching me Japanese."

## TIME PIECE

I've placed my father's wristwatch in a clear bag
and nailed it to the telephone pole.
I see it every day as I go to and from work.
Why hasn't a passerby claimed it for their own?
My father was a stickler for time—
even in the nursing home when he was half with it,
he'd check his watch and want his life on time.
One visit I couldn't set him straight
that he wasn't scheduled to box at six.

It's January and storming sleet.
I smell his cologne on a sweater I've inherited.
I approach his watch fixed to the pole.
It's still ticking. Time does not need
the warmth of a live human wrist.
Where are those slick boys I knew growing up
who could and would steal anything?

## TRUST

"You'll get a ticket parked that way," I called.
A slim black woman in cleaning clothes
that workers wear at Regions Hospital
had parked her rusty car along the curb
but pointed south, the wrong way on that street.
She smiled as if she didn't understand.
Her coat was out of style and thin
for winter here. Did she speak English?
I hesitated as she walked away—
this late I didn't want to frighten her.
"You might get towed. I wouldn't park like that."
I tapped her hood and pointed up the street.
"You show me," she said, holding out her keys.
I shook my head, astonished by her trust.
"No, no, it's not my car."
                              "You show me. Yes?"
"Okay—" I got inside uneasily
as if I put on someone else's shoes;
her large pink purse was open on the seat.
I could have driven off with everything
but swung the car around and set it right.
I dropped the ring of keys into her palm.
It clinked like a handful of poker chips.
"Good luck," I said. She smiled and off she went.
The hospital ahead was bright like a casino.

THREE

TROUBLE KNOCKING

# THE OTHER SIDE

For Vino carefully dipping
his great Belgian draft horse head
over the electric fence,
the grass on the other side
may or may not be greener
but it is much longer.

## HURRY, HURRY

Tina might as well have yelled, "Fire!"
when she hollered, "Dick's here!"
I'd need a fireman's pole to get downstairs faster.
"Hurry, hurry," Tina tells us. Her sister Barb
runs with me to the north field
where Dick's harvesting the cut hay.

Dick doesn't nod and keeps his single hand
gripping the tractor's steering wheel.
We time our leaps onto his wagon
as if we're boarding a moving boxcar
and then stack several square bales
already kicked back onto the wagon.
Dick, a nearby farmer, is still stirred up from yesterday
when his baler quit. He'd sputtered curses,
then sped his tractor with baler in tow
thirty miles late in the day to get it fixed.
The culprit, he told Tina by phone,
was the damn grapple hook I'd been using.
He wants more of her hay crop now.

On an iced-tea break in the yard,
Dick, Barb and I are joined by Tina and Teri,
a friend stacking bales with her in the barn.
We talk about the heat and little else.
I sense Dick and the rest of them expect
an explanation from me for yesterday.
I'd balked at poking my arm in the baler
to see if my missing hook had jammed it.

I'll explain myself to Dick, to all of them,
when Dick reveals how he lost his arm,
the long sleeve of his work shirt hanging
like blue drapery from his left shoulder.

## GETTING AROUND

Five o'clock, Sunday morning,
Tina and I wake to rain and clatter outside.
Our dogs—a poodle, a rat terrier,
and a huge part-retriever mutt—tear out to a ladder
extending up the side of a full wagon of hay.
They leap up like ravenous sharks.
Whoever's up there best not slip.

"Enough. No barking. Down. It's only Don."
It's Don Roberts, seventy-eight years old with a bad knee,
who in the dim morning light and rain
appears to be fifty feet up as he crawls
and pulls a plastic tarp across the hay.
"Katie! Betsy! Stella! Enough! You know Don."

He secures the tarp and climbs down,
telling us he drove over with a tarp and ladder
when he learned from Joni we ran out of time
to stack our last load of hay in the barn.

The dogs lick and nose Don's hands. He comes in
for coffee, and then he's off to deliver
vegetables in Minneapolis and then back
to the other side of Menomonie to see John the potter.

I reflect to Tina after he leaves,
"I sure hope I'm that active and getting around
when I'm Don Roberts' age."
"I don't know why you're hoping that," Tina responds.
"You're not that way now."

# TENDING THE BURN PILE

Tina lights the fire starters she's wedged
in the base of a towering pile of basswood branches,
a jumble in the west pasture we've eyed
all through the windy, rainy summer.
I'm dressed in tattered clothing
so airborne embers don't pock
my good farm jacket and jeans.

When the fire roars up,
I'm ready with a long-handle spade
to snuff hot particles that might kindle old hay
stretching on the ground like a wide fuse
from the fire to the wooden power pole,
a pole like one from my childhood
our burn barrel of leaves ignited.
Firemen luckily drenched the flames
that scorched it and our neighbor's garage.

Tina leaves me to my own decisions
as she's off to vacuum up ladybugs,
their annual house invasion lacking
the tolerable furtiveness of bats and mice.
So I start rolling toward the fire
the first of a dozen large trunk pieces,
using the long pry bar I gave her as a gift.

Tina only observed the pieces might not burn,
only remarked they might be used to thwart erosion
or perhaps become rustic patio chairs.
Patio chairs, I grumble—for the patio we toiled
to make one Saturday, lifting and laying down
concrete slab after slab, the patio
when I returned the next weekend
she'd somehow lifted up entirely to create
a walk from the house to the water pump.

# LEASHES

The dog owner at the pet hospital in Minneapolis
wearing a camouflage hunting cap
holds a long strap of a leash
as if he'd soon be off to the woods.
An attendant brings a thin brown Labrador.
The cashier tells the owner his dog has a lovely tail
and then how much he owes. I'd never pay that much
for that or any dog, I think, knowing well
I'll soon pay much more for ours.
The Lab pees red urine across the floor
and then, leashed, pulls the owner toward the door.

"Good news," the vet said, "Katie doesn't have cancer.
The bad is we're guessing it's fungal.
Biopsies and blood work are negative,
but the MRI shows nasal bones eaten away."
I agree to an infusion of clotrimazole,
an hour-long procedure under anesthesia
soaking her nose and sinuses.

Now I'm brought our dazed dog.
The cashier says, "Your poodle looks fantastic."
Katie looks cross-eyed. I pay and draw her out
on the string of a leash the clinic provides.
She wouldn't leap and run
if the whole parking lot were squirrels.
What's the recovery time
for a diagnosis we're guessing at?
The toll of further treatment?
How long will Tina and I be willing
to lead Katie along?

# COWBOY

On an early December afternoon
we free Cowboy from the corral we'd built
with fencing and metal stakes pulled from the brush.
The corral had stopped the ram
from escaping through the electric fence,
stopped him from getting shocked
and mangling the wires inoperable.

Cowboy had been pent up for months:
we didn't want the ewes birthing lambs in winter.
Tina and I hold sturdy sticks now as we open his gate.
I'm not surprised he speeds by—his thin legs churning,
supporting a body solid as a keg of beer.

He stretches his head out and zeroes in on Greta.
Earlier, she'd backed her rear up against the corral,
but his tries to mount her through the fencing failed.
He chases her around and around the sheep shed,
sniffing her behind when she slows.
I think of a line from a James Cotton song:
"You've got my nose open and I don't care."

Tina doesn't care to watch what's next
and goes back to the house. Cowboy is oblivious to me.
He's Groucho Marx hunched forward, waving a cigar
and wisecracking as women at a party flee from him.

No wonder the electric fence couldn't bolt him back.
Greta stands still now. Cowboy mounts her—
his hard penis is human in size
compared to the dangling length
the draft horse swings around.
He doesn't take long on her,
and then he's off pursuing and sniffing Velma
around and around the sheep shed.

There's no dampening his exuberance
by exhorting him to do it inside the shed
or at least for awhile appear to be monogamous.
He's doing what he's here on the farm to do.

Tina who's envisioned a large, profitable sheep herd
returns after some reflection and yells,
"Ride 'em, Cowboy!"

## COYOTES

As the red light kept blinking, warning
of a short in the electric fence,
I kept shoveling snow off the ground-level wire
and counting sheep: the ram, six ewes,
eleven lambs all present and baaing
for their morning oats and hay.

I was afraid of coyotes
after Robin saw a pack rummaging near her house.
It would take an hour of stooping and shoveling
to clear the low wire around the fenced pasture.
I couldn't tell when I talked with Tina
as she leaned out the upstairs window
if she really thought the thaw would melt the snow
or she was just too busy in the house to help.

I kept shoveling. I'd overseen the births
of four of the lambs last summer
when Tina had gone to Pierz to help her parents.
All of the lambs were as tall as the ewes now,
even Bummer, rejected at birth by his mother,
whom Tina bottle fed for three months.

Halfway around the pasture, I stooped
to adjust an insulator with my wet glove.
"Aaaaaaaaaaah! Damn it. Damn it!"
My howling sent Katie into a barking fit.
Tina opened the upstairs window and called:
"What's wrong?
Are you okay?
Is the fence working?"

# CAST ROOM

"I've got issues here," Tina told Dr. Lannon,
an affable, thirtyish orthopedist, after he prescribed
a hard cast and crutches for two to four weeks.
She broke her right ankle stacking hay.

Dr. Lannon pointed to her X-ray:
"If you choose the walking boot and it doesn't heal,
I'd have to stick pins here and wiring there."
"Excuse me, Doctor," I said, "Tina means by 'issues'
she has sheep lambing, spinach and asparagus to pick,
tomato cages to set, hours of lawn to mow, horses—"

"How long do you want the cast on?" he asked Tina,
as his nurse pushed the top of her swollen purple foot
toward her shinbone and he wrapped her lower leg
in wet blue tape. "Two weeks," she said firmly,
as firmly as she told me earlier
I had to unload the last hay wagon
before she'd even call the clinic.

"Tina," I said, "I'd go longer.
If you take the cast off, X-ray it, and it's not—"
"Two weeks is fine," Dr. Lannon said.
"My pins and wires talk was to cover myself.
It's called informed consent.
She'll be ready for a walking boot in two."

The next morning at the farm Tina and I had issues.
"Could you hang the tent up on the line?" she asked.
"It's still wet from last weekend."
"Yes," I said and moved toward the back door.
"Could you cut five or six irises for me, too?"
"Yes." I moved toward the front door.

"And fill the bird feeders?"
"Yes." The seed is in the barn out the back door.
"Before that could you run upstairs
and get my black left tennis shoe?"
"Yes." Later, back in Minneapolis,
I phoned Tina to apologize
for forgetting to cut her irises.
"I didn't remind you," she said.
"You seemed in a hurry to go."

# HARVEST TIME

I pare plums at the kitchen table,
hundreds ripening in boxes, pots, and trays
after we picked the tree clean yesterday,
depriving ants, wasps, and squirrels of their harvest.

Everything is ripening now.
"The garden waits for no one," Tina tells me.
This morning we battled time itself
as we hunched to pick cucumbers
before they grew too huge to make eatable pickles.
Last weekend we picked cherries, peaches, apricots.

From the kitchen table I see
the pear tree's branches bent, some broken,
from the weight of fruit. I see tomatoes red
in the garden ready to be picked and canned
for juice, salsa, and spaghetti sauce.

Last night I dreamed I was in Bridget's kitchen,
a woman I loved years ago but left
as my grand post-college plans did not include
marriage and children, nor did they, I might add,
include these fruits and vegetables.
Bridget has e-mailed me the last few years at work,
but I have yet to respond.

Still, in my dream I think she wouldn't mind
if I just show up in her kitchen.
Her countertop crammed with peppers, onions,
garlic, pumpkins, and squash looks familiar.
She comes in the back door with a woman friend
and a half dozen brown-haired children.

I am at her sink washing dirt off carrots.
Bridget is beautiful, much younger than the photo
she's posted on the internet.

She wears a green tank top without a bra. Her friend
makes a wisecrack about Bridget and some guy.
She hushes her and the three of us laugh.

The dream fades. The last time I saw her
we chatted in my one-room apartment
as she nursed her infant son.
Then she left to pick her husband up.
I poured whiskey into my instant coffee.

I look out Tina's kitchen window:
the horses and sheep need hay and water.
And now a farmer delivers our order
of forty slaughtered chickens we'll need
to cut up, package, and freeze.
We'll go to bed late again tonight.
Tina again will be up at dawn.

# SCHEDULED

I called to Bummer as Tina haltered him,
"Don't worry, Bummer. It's Tina.
She bottle fed you all last summer."
"Will you shut up!" Tina barked. "Just shut up."
"Okay, but I'm just trying to calm him."
Bummer was the last of five lambs we corralled
the night before so they'd load easily this morning.
We were scheduled for the slaughterhouse at nine.
Tina drew him to the trailer and I lifted him in.

The butcher at Farm and Woods Locker
directed us a mile down the road
to a rusty, one-story, unmarked building.
The door we tried opened to a worker
with a meat saw cutting a large hanging carcass.
He waved us out and around the building.

Tina backed her trailer to his coworker's signals.
He stopped her several feet from the dock, hopped
into the trailer and shoved the lambs forward.
The last two balked at leaping over and he threw them.

The dock floor was caked with dirt and dung.
"Get going! Get in there! Go on!" he yelled
as the lambs stalled at the dark entrance.
He then jumped onto the dock and pushed them in.
He continued to shout inside, "Get away from there!
Go on! Get away! Get!"

Back at the locker the butcher agreed
to all of Tina's cuts for her two lambs
and for the three she'd sold to others:
spare ribs, leg, loin and shoulder chops,
roasts, lamb burger, stew meat.

He'd make sure too she got the hearts
and other organs for dog meat.
He couldn't give her the tongues, though.
Tina persisted telling him that tongue's
the most delicious part of lamb.
"I just can't give you any," he finally said.
"It has to do with how they're shot."

# EASEMENT

The farmer who knocks at Tina's mudroom door
shows up strategically at supper time,
his green harvesting equipment
idling outside with headlights on.
The young men driving the combine
and two towering tractors with grain carts
shift in their seats, tinker with dials and gears
as if they're hoping to hell
they'll have something left of their Saturday night.

Perhaps the farmer will ask forgiveness
from a higher power on Sunday morning,
but tonight he's here to wheedle
permission out of Tina to cross her land
to harvest soy beans from a rented field.
He'd snuck the bean crop in last spring,
ignoring the NO TRESPASSING signs the sheriff advised:
five signs we'd fixed to thick, pressure-treated posts,
secured with cement and rocks
in deep holes we'd dug with shovels.

He tells us he's sorry—that he's just found out
he had no easement to cross her land,
but here's the thing: his right of way
is all grown over with poplar and birch.
He'll pay to cross—just set a price.
Did we know he cuts hay free for Carol?
Did we know he deer hunts with Jim?
Did we need venison? He's got a freezer full.

Tina refuses access to him and his machines,
tells him her fields are getting gouged and it's got to stop.
He spiels again and once again
about paying money, cutting hay free for Carol,
deer hunting with Jim—the third time adding
his machines are rented just for tonight
and his beefers need beans for the winter.

Tina concedes, tells the farmer go ahead.
We won't have to call the sheriff now, can get back
to eating the supper Tina's made of roast beef,
cabbage salad, and Mediterranean potato pie.
"Thanks, folks!" he calls as he hustles to his pickup truck.
"I'll be sure to check with you first thing next spring."
"No!" Tina yells. "This is it! There's no next spring!"
Neither the man nor his crew acknowledges hearing her
over the din of accelerating machines.

## STELLA

Tina sounded congested when I phoned last night.
"Are you getting a cold?" I asked.
"It's something else," she said and broke down crying.
"I can't talk now. Can I call you back?"
"It's okay to cry," I said. "Just tell me what's wrong."
"It's the dog. She's gone. She's dead."
"What happened? Which dog?" I asked.
"Stella," Tina said and continued crying.
"Harris killed her," she sobbed then the phone went dead.
"The person you've been speaking to—"
I called back—her phone needs a new battery.
"Hello," Tina said and the phone went dead.

She called back. "Your neighbor killed Stella?" I asked.
"She's always here. What else could have happened?
I let her out this morning and left for work.
Harris was pounding stakes on the property line.
No one else was around. What else could have happened?"
"Tina, I don't think Lloyd would do that."
"Why do you say that? Who else is there?" she asked.
"Stella shakes like Katie when she hears gunshots.
Someone's been shooting at her. Now she's gone.
When I got back, she hadn't touched her food.
She's one hundred and twenty pounds
and always cleans her bowl.
I know her howling at coyotes at night angers Harris,
but I've kept her inside the last two weeks.
He can't hear her howling in the house.

"I can't talk anymore," Tina said and started sobbing.
"The person you've been speaking to—"
I called back. "Do you want me to drive out?"
"No, I'm going to bed."
"Do you want me to phone Harris?" I asked.
"That wouldn't do much good."
"Okay, but call me if you need to. Wake me up."

65

Tina phoned me at work the next morning:
"I found Stella."
"Dead or alive?" I asked.
"I searched over the fields again and down the road.
I called, whistled, and honked like yesterday. I looked
behind the garage and barn twice. Then I found her."
"Dead or alive?" I asked.
"Alive."
"Is she okay? Where was she?"
"I pulled the garage door up," Tina said,
"and was I shocked
when that big dog came bounding out."

# RUN-UP TO TINA'S ELECTION LOSS

"Tina, Tom Nilsen calling. Bad news.
Al Weedman, the Nolan Market clerk, said no
when I asked to hang your campaign poster.
He said you're an embezzler and convicted felon.
It's all over the internet, he said, and all over town."
Tina phoned Weedman. He hung up. She called back.
He said he's busy and he'd call her later.
"Let's drive there," I said. "You'll chew on this all day."

Three customers stepped aside from the counter
as Tina and I came in. They weren't in a hurry.
"Are you Al Weedman?" Tina asked the clerk.
"Yes," he said, "I'm Al Weedman."
"I'm Tina and I'm running for Rogin Township treasurer.
You're smearing me, saying I'm a convicted felon."
"It's on the Wisconsin Court website," he said.
"No, it isn't," I said. "It isn't anywhere on the internet."
"I saw it there," he insisted. "No, you didn't," I said,
"and you're telling people Tina's a felon."
"Who told you I'm telling people?" he countered.
"You've told people it's all over town," I said.
"How's my last name spelled?" Tina asked.
"What is my last name?" she continued.
"I don't recall," Weedman replied.
"Then why are you lying about me?"

We laid it on about defamation of character,
maligning and slandering, taking legal action.
We were about to shoot our last futile arrow
about bearing false witness against thy neighbor
in this supposedly Christian town
when Weedman gave in, promised
he'd stop telling people Tina was a felon.
I went fuming to the car, but Tina
chatted up his lingering customers
and asked for their votes on Tuesday.

## TROUBLE KNOCKING

A living room light turns on
as I walk down the yard to the farmhouse.
I see Tina in her red plaid nightgown.
Katie isn't barking, but she's a white blur
running back and forth from door to window.

She must have awakened Tina when I greeted Stella,
the watch dog out here, who didn't bark either
but bounded to my car as if nothing were odd
seeing me this late and in the middle of the week.

Tina stands back from the door
as if trouble were about to knock.
I am a dark figure approaching the house.
I call to her, "Tina, it's me. It's Kevin. I'm Kevin."

She's expressionless and doesn't move,
but asks through the closed glass door,
as Katie paws it excitedly,
"What are you doing here?"

"I drove out to see if you were okay.
I told you I'd call tonight.
Your phone's been busy since five o'clock.
The operator said no one was on the line."

Tina turns toward the living room,
apparently sees the phone askew,
and lets me in. I kiss her but we don't embrace.
"I thought you said maybe you'd call," she says.

In the morning, as I drive to work from the farm,
I realize how wary I'd be if Tina,
the woman I've loved for many years,
appeared unexpectedly in the city
knocking late at night.

# HOBBY FARM

After reaching from a ladder all Saturday afternoon
to harvest the cherry tree, I understand
why the boy George Washington
chopped down his father's tree.

In the barn
I collect eighteen eggs from the nesting boxes
then muse on the origin of the Easter egg hunt
as I climb the round hay bales to search for eggs
two of the twenty hens habitually lay up there.

Out in the garden
I pick the onions, garlic, radishes, and spinach
Tina needs to prepare supper.
"You know," she reflects, "making
homemade pizza isn't easy
when you grow your own ingredients."

The electric water pump goes out.
I phone Jerome from Beaver Creek.
He arrives in his pickup blaring music about Jesus.
His bumper stickers declare:
VEGETARIAN IS AN INDIAN WORD FOR POOR HUNTER,
THE BEST HOMELAND DEFENSE IS AN ARMED CITIZEN.

He scares me, but he gets the pump working,
just like he fixed the riding lawn mower,
baled the north field before it rained
when our tractor broke down,
and gave us his extra tire-changing ramp
in case the horse trailer had a flat.

Back home in Minneapolis
two neighbors pause in their grumbling about yardwork
as I unload my weekend of stuff.
"Is Tina's farm a real farm or a hobby farm?" one calls.

"Good question," I call back.
"On a scale from playing Scrabble
to winter surfing on Lake Superior,
what's your idea of a hobby?"

# FOUR

# STAYING PUT

# OVERTIME

I phoned the claimant Sunday afternoon
and he was up. I had to find out when
he'd quit his job to set his benefits.
He wheezed and coughed and drew on oxygen.
"I worked until the biopsy came back,"
then what he said next made both of us laugh.
"You're working Sundays?" "Yes, on overtime."
"Well, damn, I hope you're getting time and a half."

Monday at coffee break I quipped to friends
I'd left the farm early for overtime
as if performing an illicit act.
Ruth jumped on me as if it were a crime.
I parried her persistence with a smile
and said, "I'm working through my middle age
without Prozac or pricey therapy.
I'll need some dough when I get through this stage."

"I've only got so many summers," Ruth replied—
she's sixty now and won't work extra hours.
"So much I'd love to do from reading books—
I've stacks I want to read—to raising flowers,
golf, hikes, bird watching, visiting. You know,
I wouldn't have to leave the state—it's all
right here. If I could win the lottery—
even a little one—I'd quit and have a ball."

## UP

No one punched me in the nose.
My bandage covers the site
where abnormal skin was surgically removed.
"Everything should be fine," my doctor said,
but he's ordered further testing.

At home I scrutinize my face in the mirror:
I think of the bronze, hollowed-out husk of a bee
I swept up from the kitchen floor
and exhibit on a sheet of paper.

Then I think of my eighty-eight-year-old mother
in a nursing home now for rehab
because she stopped getting out of bed.
"I am an invalid," my mother exclaimed to the staff
of physical and occupational therapists,
but they were harder of hearing than she.

When I visited her today,
she was eager to show me how to rise up in a walker.
Scooting forward to the end of her bed,
she positioned her feet well beneath her on the floor,
gripped the walker's handles,
and started to somersault forward.

Up she went
rising into her walker.
It worked.
I tried it myself.
Up I went.

## JUNE AFTERNOON

I'm watching Tina's farm this weekend while she's away.
It's another hot, dry, quiet afternoon in June.
I've pulled the hose to a scraggly pear tree
to soak it slowly for an hour or so.

Meanwhile, like a vigilant parent expecting visitors,
I brush Vino's tangled, cream-colored mane and soiled tail.
He cooperates with my fussiness, awaiting an oat reward
from the metal container in the barn, tightly

lidded due to sparrows swooping in and out—
birds that farmers out here call flying mice.
"Another hot one!"—a wiry, middle-aged man startles me.
He'd parked his silver Dodge Ram up by the mailbox.

I ready for questions this stranger in a blue seed cap
might ask: "Are you the land owner?" "No," I'll say,
"and Tina's not here." "Does she rent out her fields? ...
Do her woods need cutting? ... Can I deer hunt this fall? ...
Is she married?"

That last question always catches me. I'd be rude out here
to ask him why he asks. "I'll have her call you," I'll say,
take his number, return to my June afternoon,
give Vino oats, grumble about sparrows,
pull the hose to a parched plum tree.

## THE EASY PART

Tina stood ready with the sheep hoof knife.
Emma had been limping in the field
and needed her hooves inspected, cleaned, and pared
in the tight pen we had built for this.
I had the easy part according to the sheep manual.
I'd position myself on Emma's left side,
turn her head far to the right with my left hand,
and press down on her right hip with my right hand.
When she rolled to the ground, I'd raise
her front legs and head and balance her on her rump.

Emma, a low, wide, rotund ewe, didn't budge.
She was as immobile as a Sumo wrestler.
I tried to finesse her again and again.
We couldn't give in as her hooves if infected
could lead to foot rot. I hunched over her from behind,
gripped her by the shoulders, and lifted up
as Tina crawling beneath her pulled her back legs forward.
Emma plopped back on top of me and we hit the ground.
Tina noticed the two plastic shopping bags
I'd fixed with rubber bands over my hiking shoes.
"Why don't you wear the rubber boots I bought you?
A neighbor could drive up."

"Because I'd still have to scrape off sheep poop," I said.
I got up and resumed the manual's technique,
raised Emma on her rump
and held her front legs from behind
as Tina dug dirt out and pared her long narrow hooves.
I saw the focus in Tina's face, so I said to both of them,
"Where did it all go wrong? I'm too important for this.
I should have gone to therapy ten years ago."
Tina replied, "Let's buy that sheep deck chair
the manual suggests. Hand me the dewormer plunger."
"Baaaa, baaaa," Emma cried.

# MIDWINTER THAW

Invigorated by days of warmth
when temperatures shot from ten below to fifty above,
Tina built a seedling light station on her farm
to start her onions, lettuce, broccoli, and peas.
These she'd plant as soon as she could till.

I kept quiet as I recalled
the year she started her tomato seeds too soon
and had to plant the tall seedlings in mid-May.
When hit by a cold snap, she scrambled to save them,
donning each with a white foam cup. None survived.
Her garden looked like a military cemetery.

In the city the recent warm spell
melted into memory the ice dams on my roof
that I could barely dent with a hand pick.
Animal life—rabbit, raccoon, turkey, coyote—
ranged in the dark over the residual snow.

I kept my winter cap and coat on
as I hiked along the river parkway in the afternoon
amidst joggers, bicyclists, and family outings:
all in a lightly clad march toward spring.

I felt like the lost gray cat
I found meowing in a dim recess of my garage
as I left for work. It must have slipped out
on some distracted owner one warm day.

Despite my calls of "Here, nice kitty, kitty,"
the cat hunkered in its niche of security
under a shelf on the concrete floor
as if I were a hawk hovering over it.

The next morning
the forecast was for snow and more snow.
The cat in the garage had split. Tina phoned from the farm
her seedlings were growing so fast
she'd need to plant them in a few weeks at most.

"Do you know the weather?" she asked.
"No, not really," I said.

# TIES THAT BIND

Our employee handbook calls us family,
a warm, endearing, but confining term:
the thought of playing wedding shower games
like being wrapped in toilet paper makes me squirm.
And what if as coworker family members
we eye each other with lascivious desires
leading to consensual, incestuous groping
and ending publicly in massive fires?

I know when I retire or out and quit,
I won't come visiting. That's how it's been
past jobs: the whole work-family thing recedes
in my mind's rearview mirror to way back then.
Reputed mothers, fathers, siblings, sons
and daughters, aunts and uncles are left behind
as I'm accelerating through the present,
relieved to have cut free the ties that bind.

But say someday I need to make a visit
to retrieve forgotten stuff or sign a form,
I'll call ahead—no one can just show up:
the doors are locked, security's the norm.
My former sister Fran will peer through glass,
allowing entry once she's checked her list.
I'll think of laughs we had on breaks as she
fastens an ID bracelet on my wrist.

# MEMENTO

When she was diagnosed as terminal,
my neighbor tagged her valuables with names
of family and friends. All her antiques
and knickknacks—culled from garage and rummage sales
to grace three floors of rooms—now pulled her down.

At her request her brother came each week
to weed her vegetables after she died.
She fretted that people on their way to church
would gossip that her garden was unkempt.

On the estate sale's final day I finger
*101 Strings Perform Bob Dylan*
and think of things of mine that I might toss.
"Let's get together soon," she'd always say,
"when life slows down a bit." We never did.

Tonight as a memento I will pluck
a prize tomato ripe red off her vine.
Tomorrow the new owners have hired men
to lay the garden low and pour cement.

# MOHS SURGERY WAITING ROOM

A man sitting across from me squints
as he leans forward on his cane.
He had Mohs surgery right after me.
We're waiting for results.
He wears khaki pants and a gray tee shirt
over his protruding stomach. He looks like a worker
who hasn't worked for sometime, a worker left behind
when the appliance factory moved overseas.

"Kevin," he calls, "I'm Pete."
I'm still wearing my office ID
and feel like a tagged sheep on Tina's farm.
He points to the white bandages on our foreheads
and proclaims, "No biggie."
His "No biggie" unsettles me
as if he'd unsealed a jar of rice
releasing a swarm of flies around me.
He doesn't know my deep margins biopsy,
doesn't know my last time here
I was back and forth to Room 1
all morning for surgeries on my ear.

I nod his way then ask,
"Did you hurt your knee, Pete?"
"Below the knee amputations," he responds.
"Wow. No walker even. How do you do it?"
"I promised my ex after my second amp
I'd mow her lawn and catch her fish as always.
I've got a pontoon, pack a lunch and diet pop,
and I'm good for the day."

"Mr. FitzPatrick," my surgery nurse calls,
"Dr. Reed will see you in Room 2."
"Do you know what 2 means?" Pete exclaims.
"No biggie," I concede.

## VALENTINE'S DAY

"I'd like a dozen medium stem roses,"
I tell the clerk, a teenager with pigtails.
"What color?" she asks. "We've got red, yellow,
peach, pink, pink with red edging—
they're very, very beautiful—and even green."
"Green roses?" I ask. "Yes, a kind of mint green."
"I don't see them," I say. "Oh, they're in back.
I'm not even allowed to touch them yet—
this is only my first week. I love flowers."

As the roses I've chosen are being wrapped,
I want to tell the new clerk who loves flowers
that the woman these roses are for loves flowers too.
And how obtuse I was about this until a delivery man
brought roses to our house in Minneapolis.
Tina just glowed, but then he returned apologizing
that the order was for the next block over.
I'd never seen such joy in her or disappointment.
I buy her roses now each Valentine's Day.

But the floral shop is busy;
I don't want to slow the clerk down.
I remind her to add baby's breath and ferns,
then I step back into the long, snowy winter
and drive to Tina's farm, heartened
by pink with red-edged roses.

## NAVIGATOR, NEXT
*In Tina's voice*

I woke to Stella's barking outside.
It wasn't her usual howling.
Both security lights were on. Someone was here.
I looked down from my bedroom window:
a young woman wearing a gold necklace,
a white sleeveless blouse, and capri pants
knocked at the kitchen door.
Katie ran downstairs barking.

"Who is it?" I called from the window.
"Is this Boaz?" she asked. "Who? Where?" I said.
"Boaz. I'm looking for the town of Boaz."
"Both? How do you spell it?"
"B-O-A-Z," she said.
"Boaz! That's fifty miles from here."
"I'm from out East. My GPS says this is Boaz.
But, whatever, can I crash on your couch?"
"Your what?" I asked. "Your compass?"
"My global positioning system," she said.

"This is a farm. Don't you have a map?"
I shouted over Katie's ceaseless barking. Damn poodles.
"Just my GPS," she said.
I said nothing more. It was two in the morning.
She wore summer clothes on a cool April night.
Her silver SUV beneath the garage security light
was a shiny UFO with tinted windows
descended on my property.
There could be others inside.
"All right," she said. "I'll sleep in my vehicle."

Katie stopped barking.
I fell asleep though I didn't think I could.
At four Stella started again outside,
the security lights went on,

Katie ran around the bedroom barking.
The woman drove her SUV by the house
straight toward my electric fence for the sheep.

"That's not a road!" I yelled down at her.
I could hear her say, "Navigator, next," and then
"My commander tells me this is the road to Boaz."
"Stop. You'll drive through my fence. Stop!"

"Well, what's the proper way out?" she asked.
"Back, back from where you came."
She reversed her SUV, backing it slowly
in stops and starts up the drive.
I could hear her say, "Navigator, repeat.
Navigator, next. Navigator, previous."

She got up to the mailbox finally,
turned her vehicle toward the highway and stars
and disappeared.

# QUESTIONING

Fifty white chickens
being raised for meat not eggs
push every which way against
the wire mesh coop gate
that restrains them from getting out
and running over, under, and around me
as I fill their five long trays
with a quart each of Meat Maker poultry feed.

On Friday morning, the first day of Tina's
three-day horseback riding trip,
I forgot her fill-the-feeders-first advice.
Now I unlatch the gate and step aside
as the chickens trample past me
like frantic shoppers at a 7:00 a.m. sale.
I set one obese chicken on its feet
who'd been flailing on its back like a flipped turtle.

On Sunday afternoon when Tina returns,
I describe the feeding comedy to her in detail.
"How much Meat Maker did they get?" she asks.
"One quart in each of the five trays, three times a day."
"You were starving them," she says. "I told you
four quarts per tray two times a day."

She then shifts her focus
from questioning my animal husbandry
to figuring how to fit in my Honda Civic
four large coolers of frozen chicken and lamb.
She hasn't forgotten the long deep freezer
she left me in Minneapolis years ago.

I hope the authorities don't pull me over
and ask me what do I know,
where have I been,
where am I going.

## BOBCAT SKID-STEER LOADER

Tina climbs into her Bobcat skid-steer loader
wearing a coyote fur bomber hat,
a bulky, thermal-lined farm jacket,
and knee-high rubber boots
that boast "Polar Proven" on the sides.
She hoots as she starts on the first try
the touchy, unmuffled diesel engine.
We could be characters in a *Fargo* sequel.

I latch the hay-bale spear attachment—
a long, hard, shiny tool. Tina pivots the Bobcat
and thrusts the spear deep into the center
of an eight-hundred-pound round bale of hay.
I hurry ahead opening and shutting gates
as she drives the bale out to the pasture.

I am an attendant now.
"Any man could do this," I think.
I thought that too on hot summer afternoons
when I stacked square bales in the barn,
and on cold winter mornings when I pulled bales
out to the sheep on a long plastic sled.
"Any man could do this," I'd think,
but I'd also think, "Would any man want to do this?"

We won't have much hard farm labor anymore.
Tina has a catalog of Bobcat attachments
offering to do just about anything—shear trees,
crush rocks, grind stumps, whatever.

I make myself useful
picking burs from Katie's paws and ears as Tina returns,
driving toward us up a steep, snow-packed hill.
Halfway up the Bobcat rocks back, front tires in the air.
She's stuck and could flip.
"Pivot around," I yell. "Come up in reverse."

At the top of the hill
Tina looks at me in amazement and says,
"That's the best suggestion you've made yet."

# FAREWELL

"Ahoy! It's Captain Bob calling
with free boarding passes for all."
I talk back as the recorded message rattles on.
"It's a miracle you have my cell phone number,
Captain Bob. I rarely give it out.
I expected Tina when 'Fur Elise' went off.

"I don't know what your time or weather is.
I'm on top of a snowy hill on a Wisconsin farm.
I'm burying our dog Katie.
She's in rigor mortis and has a bloody ass.
It's getting dark, Captain Bob.
She felt as light as a cardboard cutout
when I lifted her on the sled and pulled her here.

"I shoveled snow away, laid her on some towels,
and put her bunny under her head for a pillow.
I'm piling rocks on top of her, Captain Bob.
It's March, the earth is frozen,
I don't want her chewed on by scavengers
like a deer carcass along the highway.

"Should we get another white standard poodle,
Captain Bob, and call her Katie?
Should we just suck it in? She was twelve years old,
for Christ's sake, almost thirteen.
A neighbor down the road just had a stroke.

"I'm scraping for more rocks—
she's so stretched out and it's getting darker.
Captain Bob, it's a miracle you have my cell phone number.
I don't want any free boarding passes,
but could you grant Katie and me one hour
to return to Tina and the lit farmhouse
as if we were out on an evening hike?

"'Katie, down,' I'll say when we enter the mudroom,
and she'll drop until she hears the creak of my chair.
Then she'll sneak over to nuzzle my hand
and pry it up with her long nose
until I stroke her head and ears,
under her chin and down her neck and back.

"When it's time, Captain Bob,
I'll whisper, 'Katie, what's that? Who's out there?'
She'll run barking to the mudroom door. I'll open it
and she'll charge off the back steps
toward that dark, snowy, wooded hill
to chase off for all of us whatever's out there.
'Good dog,' I'll call. 'Katie, you're a good dog.'"

# GOOD HAY

"Darrell's stealing from us!" Tina bursts over the phone.
"You've got to call him. He won't answer my calls."
I'm silent, having just stepped in the door from work.
"You mean you won't help me?"
"What exactly do you want me to say?" I ask.

I tell Darrell I'm Tina's husband, tell him what we want.
"Sir, I have to disagree," Darrell responds.
"That hay is perfectly fine. My cattle would eat it.
I'll bale the hay I've cut in your fields,
but that's the hay you're getting.
I know good hay, sir, and that's good hay."

I call Tina and then call Darrell.
I call Tina and then call Darrell.
"Darrell, again, Tina says the hay stinks.
It's moldy. You've left it lying too long.
She wants hay her horses would eat—twelve
one-thousand-pound round bales of good hay—
or you can just leave our share and yours."
"You can't leave cut hay, sir," Darrell says.
"You'll wreck your fields."

I unpack my briefcase as I update Tina.
I try to calm her, ask her to describe
her sunset—my view in the city is blocked
by a neighbor's enormous garage. She describes
clouds reflecting the red of the setting sun
and a sky of pinks and blues in horizontal lines
over the hilly west pasture. She thanks me
for calling Darrell and for calling back.

Darrell's partner stops at the farm the next morning.
Tina agrees to swap the cut hay with them
for ten one-thousand-pound round bales,
only if each is leafy, fine-stemmed, and doesn't smell.

# STAYING PUT

My ear plugs are some help at three in the morning
when Tina unable to sleep gets up
to scrape out the wood stove, clunk in new firewood,
blend yogurt and berries, wash a load of clothes.

My sleep-inducing rituals—
repeating a mantra or prayers embedded since childhood,
counting down by sevens from one hundred—
bring no relief as I ponder whether religion
began not in the awareness of change and death
but in insomnia—the counting of imaginary sheep
the first crude prayer.

I could rise to grind coffee beans, vacuum,
scrub the mudroom floor in moonlight,
a whirl of extraterrestrial energy,
but I'd just be underfoot like Betsy
lying near Tina's feet like a speed bump
when she's busy cooking and the phone rings.
"Damn dog! Out—you're going outside now!"

It's safer, warmer for me to stay put,
practicing replies I might need on rising
to deflect any early morning plans
Tina's caffeinated self might concoct for me—
getting a puppy for company in the city,
buying Vino and learning to ride,
selling apples on the highway when I retire.

Confident my replies—"Perhaps,"
"We'll see," "I'll let you know"—
would all delay well enough,
I adjust my ear plugs and sing to myself
a hopefully mesmerizing round
of "Ninety-nine bottles of beer on the wall,
ninety-nine bottles of beer …"

# GIDDYUP

Tina, my patient horseback riding teacher,
instructs me to shake a pan of oats
to lure Vino from pasture to halter to hitching post—
a trick, I note, TV cowboys never need:
their horses parked outside the saloon
ready to ride like motorcycles.

And I'm not to leap on Vino's bare back,
grab his mane and yell, "Giddyup!"
as I slap his enormous draft horse rump.
I get it—I've seen him and Ozzie bolt:
the two in my trust one Sunday afternoon
grazed untied on the lawn
when a tractor backfired and they took off
into Barrett's tall, green, August corn,
trampling up and down at stampede speed.

I follow all Tina's dos and don'ts:
brush Vino's back and underside of grit and burs,
let him smell the saddle pad, let him know it's coming,
scratch his withers, swing up the saddle,
pat his underside so he isn't alarmed,
let him know the cinches are coming,
etcetera, or what I recall of etcetera.

So Vino and I chug along in the training ring,
my muddled use of reins and boots
directing him to go two ways at once.
Tina and I were to be trail riding by now,
a fun, summer activity with other couples.
I lean forward, pat Vino's neck and swear to him,
"I'm not a quitter, Vino. I will never quit."
Luckily, he's not a talking horse like Mister Ed.

## ABOUT THE AUTHOR

Kevin FitzPatrick was educated at the University of Minnesota and the University of Saint Thomas. For many years he was the editor of the *Lake Street Review*, a Minneapolis and Saint Paul literary magazine. He is the author of two previous books of poetry, *Down on the Corner* and *Rush Hour*, both from Midwest Villages & Voices. *Greatest Hits*, a chapbook of his poetry, was published by Pudding House Publications. About his poetry Meridel LeSueur wrote, "He is a wonderful chronicler of the people's journey." Besides magazines, newspapers, and other media, his poetry has appeared in anthologies such as *American Voices: Webs of Diversity* (Prentice Hall), *Orpheus and Company: Contemporary Poems on Greek Mythology* (University of New England Press), *Call Down the Moon: Poems of Music* (Margaret K. McElderry Books), *The Next Parish Over: A Collection of Irish-American Writing* (New Rivers Press), and *Ringing in the Wilderness: Selections from the North Country Anvil* (Holy Cow! Press). FitzPatrick's poetry has been heard on *The Writer's Almanac with Garrison Keillor* and on *Weekend Edition* over Minnesota Public Radio and other public radio stations. He has read his poetry in the *Lowertown Reading Jam Series* with Carol Connolly, Ethna McKiernan, and others, and videos of these readings, recorded by the Saint Paul Neighborhood Network, are available online.

MIDWEST VILLAGES & VOICES

PROSE

*Every Woman Has a Story*, edited by Gayla Ellis
*Winter Prairie Woman*, by Meridel LeSueur
*Irene: Selected Writings of Irene Paull*, edited by Gayla Ellis et al.

POETRY

*Payments Due*, by Carol Connolly
*Payments Due: Onstage Offstage*, by Carol Connolly
*The Necklace*, by Florence Chard Dacey
*Heart, Home & Hard Hats*, by Sue Doro
*Down on the Corner*, by Kevin FitzPatrick
*Rush Hour*, by Kevin FitzPatrick
*Rites of Ancient Ripening*, by Meridel LeSueur
*This With My Last Breath*, by Meridel LeSueur
*Caravan*, by Ethna McKiernan